Cecilia

Singing and Sharing the Faith

> **Died in the Third Century**
> **Lived in Rome, Italy**
> **Feast Day: November 22**
> **Community Role: Musician**

Text by Barbara Yoffie
Illustrated by Jeff Albrecht

Liguori
ONE LIGUORI DRIVE
LIGUORI MO 63057-9999

Dedication

To my family:
my parents Jim and Peg,
my husband Bill,
our son Sam and daughter-in-law Erin,
and our precious grandchildren
Ben, Lucas, and Andrew

To all the children I have had the privilege of
teaching throughout the years.

Imprimi Potest:
Stephen T. Rehrauer, CSsR, Provincial
Denver Province, the Redemptorists

Published by Liguori Publications
Liguori, Missouri 63057

To order, visit Liguori.org or call 800-325-9521.

p ISBN 978-0-7648-2556-9
e ISBN 978-0-7648-7007-1

Liguori Publications, a nonprofit corporation, is an apostolate of the
Redemptorists. To learn more about the Redemptorists, visit Redemptorists.com.

Printed in the United States of America
19 18 17 16 15 / 5 4 3 2 1
First Edition

Dear Parents and Teachers:

Saints and Me! is a series of children's books about saints, with six books in each set. The first set, *Saints of North America,* honors holy men and women who blessed and served the land we call home. The second set, *Saints of Christmas*, includes heavenly heroes who inspire us through Advent and Christmas and teach us to love the Infant Jesus. The third set, *Saints for Families*, introduces saints who modeled God's love within and for the domestic Church.

Saints for Communities explores six individuals from different times and places who served Jesus through their various roles and professions. Saint John Baptist de la Salle taught children and founded a familiar educational system. Saint Joan of Arc helped to bring peace to the country of France. The Apostle Matthew was a tax collector before deciding to follow Jesus. The Apostle Thomas preached and built churches. Saint Cecilia sang hymns to Jesus in her heart. And Michael the Archangel is well-known for his protection.

Which saint doubted Jesus' resurrection? Which one fought a heavenly battle? Which saint heard heavenly voices? Who sold everything he owned? Which saint was first named Levi? Which saint was married against her will? Find out in the *Saints for Communities* set—part of the *Saints and Me!* series—and help your child connect to the lives of the saints.

Introduce your children or students to the *Saints and Me!* series as they:

—**READ** about the lives of the saints and are inspired by their stories.

—**PRAY** to the saints for their intercession.

—**CELEBRATE** the saints and relate them to their lives.

saints of communities

 John Baptist
Teacher

 Joan of Arc
Soldier

 Matthew
Banker

 Thomas
Construction worker

 Cecilia
Musician

 Michael
Police officer

Cecilia lived a long time ago, just a few hundred years after Jesus. She was born in Rome, Italy, to wealthy Christian parents. She was a faithful Christian, friendly, and kind. She liked to talk to other Christians about Jesus. Sometimes they would meet together and pray.

Cecilia and her family had to be careful. It was against the law to be a Christian. The Romans wanted everyone to worship Roman gods, not Jesus. Christians were put to death for their faith. But Cecilia was brave. She made a special promise to love Jesus with her whole heart.

In those days, parents planned their daughter's wedding. Cecilia's parents did not know about the promise she made to Jesus. They told her, "We have chosen Valerian to be your husband. He is very kind and good." Cecilia was sad. She knew Valerian was not a Christian.

The day of the wedding arrived. Friends came to see Cecilia marry Valerian. There was music and dancing. But Cecilia was very quiet. She was thinking about Jesus. In her heart she heard another song of joy. *"Jesus, I love you!"* she thought to herself.

Later, when Cecilia and Valerian were alone, she told him her secret: "I love Jesus with all my heart. Long ago, I promised Jesus I would always be holy and pure. Pray with me, and you will understand." He was so moved by her faith and love that he became a Christian, too!

Valerian told his brother about the Christian faith: "Jesus loves all people. He died for us." Soon Valerian's brother was baptized, too. This made Cecilia very happy!

The two brothers helped Christians nearby and prayed with them. They gave food and money to the poor. When other Christians were killed, they buried them with care. It was a dangerous job.

One day Valerian and his brother were caught burying a Christian and arrested. "You must be Christians," the soldiers shouted. "Worship our gods and we will let you go free." But they would not worship the Roman gods. They believed in Jesus.

Valerian and his brother were martyred for their faith. When Cecilia heard the sad news, she cried. She buried her husband and his brother. Some friends came to her house and prayed with her. "I know they are in heaven," said Cecilia.

Like her family, Cecilia taught others about Jesus and the Christian faith. People liked to hear about Jesus. They liked to pray with Cecilia and other Christians. Many were baptized. One day, soldiers came to her house. "You must come with us," they said. Cecilia was arrested because she was a Christian.

At first, Cecilia was afraid. The soldiers were mean. They shouted at her, "Worship our gods!" "I cannot. I love Jesus," she answered.

Cecilia was sentenced to death. The soldiers locked her in a room full of hot steam, but Cecilia was not hurt! This made the soldiers angry. One soldier hit Cecilia three times with his sword. He walked away and left her to die.

Cecilia's love and faith in Jesus were very strong. He gave her the courage she needed to live and share her faith with others. Jesus was in her heart, like a happy song that never ends.

The Church honors Cecilia as a martyr. Many wonderful stories are told about her holy life. Many churches are named after her, and she is seen in paintings, stained-glass windows, mosaics, and sculptures. Her symbols are an organ, a harp, and other musical instruments. Cecilia is the patron of church music, musicians, and singers.

Keep a song in your heart,
and a prayer in your mind.
Always be faithful, loving, and kind.

Dear Jesus.
I love you very much.
Saint Cecilia loved you
with her whole heart.
She was holy and pure.
Help me to grow
in faith and love.
With the whole
church.
I sing your praises.
Amen.

NEW WORDS (Glossary)

Christian: One who follow Jesus Christ; one who believes and follows his teachings

Courage: Carrying on in spite of danger or trouble; being unafraid

Martyr: Someone who gives up his or her life for a belief or cause

Mosaic: A picture made from small pieces of glass, stone, or tile

Sculpture: Three-dimensional artwork; a statue

Worship: To give praise or honor to God or a god